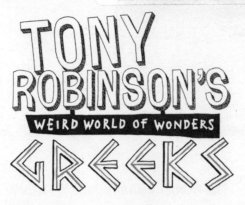

# TONY ROBINSON'S
## WEIRD WORLD OF WONDERS
# GREEKS

**Tony Robinson** has been scribbling away since he was old enough to pick up a pencil. He's written long stuff (last year he wrote a history of Australia), and shorter stuff (like this). He's rewritten old stories (like the ones about the Greek heroes Odysseus and Theseus), and made up new ones (for instance his children's TV series *Tales from Fat Tulip's Garden*). But history is what he likes best, because he says, 'How do you know who you are if you don't know where you came from?' That's why he's written Tony Robinson's Weird World of Wonders, and he doesn't want to stop until he's written about every single bit of history there's ever been - although in order to do this he'll have to live till he's 8,374!

**Del Thorpe** has been drawing ever since that time he ruined his mum's best tablecloth with wax crayons. Most of his formative work can be found in the margins of his old school exercise books. His maths teacher described these misunderstood wo[rks] [...] [sch]ool, Del [...] [grow]n-up thi[...] [...] was mo[...] [crayo]ns and [...]

# Other books by Tony Robinson

# TONY ROBINSON'S

## WEIRD WORLD OF WONDERS

# GREEKS

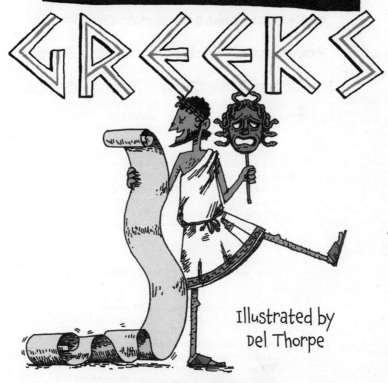

Illustrated by
Del Thorpe

MACMILLAN CHILDREN'S BOOKS

**Jessica Cobb** did the research for this book. She's a bit like Jojo in the Curiosity Crew, although she's older, cleverer and much bigger (Jojo's only 2cm* tall). Apart from that they're identical, except that Jess has two heads to store all her brains in. Thanks once again for all your hard work.

*Actually I'm nearly 3 cm tall!*

The real Nits wishes to dedicate this book to **Louise Robinson**, because Louise feeds her when she's hungry, takes her for walks, cuddles her when they watch telly and tells her off when she gets silly. Actually she does the same to me too, so I'll dedicate the book to Louise as well.

First published 2012 by Macmillan Children's Books
a division of Macmillan Publishers Limited
20 New Wharf Road, London N1 9RR
Basingstoke and Oxford
Associated companies throughout the world
www.panmacmillan.com

ISBN 978-0-330-53388-1

Text copyright © Tony Robinson 2012
Illustrations copyright © Del Thorpe 2012

The right of Tony Robinson and Del Thorpe to be identified as the
author and illustrator of this work has been asserted by them in accordance
with the Copyright, Designs and Patents Act 1988.

1 3 5 7 9 8 6 4 2

A CIP catalogue record for this book is available from
the British Library.

Typeset by Dan Newman/Perfect Bound Ltd
Printed and bound by CPI Group (UK) Ltd, Croydon CR0 4YY

**Hi! We're the Curiosity Crew. You'll spot us hanging around in this book checking stuff out.**

It's about ancient Greece, a place full of myth and legend, olive oil and nude athletics.

It was also the birthplace of big brainboxes, mad scientists and war-crazy Spartans.

Read on to find out . . .

# SWIMMING IN SOUP

**C**ongratulations! You saved up your pocket money for five whole weeks and have now finally bought the book of your dreams – *Tony Robinson's Ancient Greeks*.

Am I right?

No?

OK. You wrote a long list of all the fabulous presents you wanted for your birthday and top of that list was this book.

Wrong again?

Did you find it in a wheelie bin?

Did it drop into your hands from a passing spacecraft?

Well, however you got hold of it – you're really, really curious to turn the page and find out what it's all about, aren't you?

*Aren't you?*

Go on, dive in!

Brilliant! You did it!

You've just followed in the footsteps of the ancient Greeks.

How?

Because just like you, the Greeks wanted to find out about things. They spent tons of time asking questions, arguing, poking stuff with sticks and testing things till they broke.

And by doing this, they came up with all sorts of inventions and discoveries – from an early computer to a laser death ray! (I'm not joking).

Homer was a blind poet who told really exciting tales. His story about the war between the Greeks and the Trojans is probably the oldest to have been written down anywhere in Europe. There are older stories in other parts of the world, but most of them are pretty boring. The great thing about Homer is that all his characters seem so real, and they have such scary adventures. There is one in which the hero Odysseus (pronounced 'Odd-iss-yuss') has been trapped in a cave with all his sailors by a one-eyed giant, who starts eating them one at a time. Will Odysseus escape, or will he end up as a spoonful of mincemeat in the mouth of a foul-breathed giant . . . ?

You'll just have to read the story and find out, won't you!

The Greeks were among the first people in the world to use money, study history, work out complicated sums and write music.

Loads of things that we do today are because of the ancient Greeks.

# FROGS ON A POND

OK! So you're probably wondering who these Greeks were.

Look at this map.

It's full of dots, isn't it? Lots of little islands and cities dotted around the Mediterranean Sea.

Ancient Greece wasn't really a country. It was a collection of island-states and city-states. Some of them were famous like Athens, Sparta, and Knossos, but there were lots of others too.

Each state was its own little country with its own way of doing things. They banded together in times of crisis but they also spent a lot of time squabbling with each other!

The main bit of Greece is very rocky and difficult to farm, so most Greeks lived on the coast or on islands, where they could make money from the sea by trading or fishing.

One Greek writer said the Greeks were like *'frogs sitting around a pond'.*

Which seems a pretty good description to me – that is, if frogs wore cute little tunics and were good at philosophy and maths.

So how did ancient Greece start?

Well, in order to answer that, we'll have to dive in a bit deeper.

## GREEK SOUP

People started living in Greece more than 8,000 years ago, but annoyingly they didn't begin writing anything down for another 4,000 years.

So all we're left with from the earliest days of the Greeks are little bits of stories, legends and archaeology.

Get your cossie on.

Hurry up, girls!

Looking back into ancient Greek history is like peering into a big bowl of thick soup – bits of food float to the surface but you can't see the bottom of the bowl.

Imagine if you were swimming around in a bowl of Greek soup, with lots of ancient stories and bits of information bobbing up around you.

**MYTH:** Once upon a time a powerful king called Minos ruled the city-state of Knossos. In his huge palace was a giant maze, and at its heart lived a terrible monster.

**FACT:** In the rubble where Knossos once stood, archaeologists have found the remains of a gigantic palace that would have been home to a powerful Greek ruler around 1500 BC. It's got more than 13,000 interconnecting rooms, passages and staircases.

Sounds a bit maze-like to me! Maybe that's where the idea of the giant maze came from.

**MYTH:** One day the Prince of Athens went to a friend's wedding. A gang of creatures called centaurs who were half-man and half-horse burst in, drank all the wine and tried to kidnap the bride. But the prince drew his sword and defeated them.

Maybe this tale comes from the time when the Greeks first came into contact with horse-riding nomads. Imagine if you'd never seen one before. He'd look like a man and a horse glued together, wouldn't he?

So, sounds like these ancient cities really were rich.

MYTH: The son of the King of Troy stole the wife of the King of Sparta. The Spartan king was very angry and asked his brother, the mighty King of Mycenae, to help him get his wife back.

FACT: In the nineteenth century some incredible golden masks were found buried on a hillside in Mycenae. They were more than 3,000 years old.

MYTH: The Greeks launched a thousand ships which sailed to Troy and laid siege to it. The two armies fought for ten long years before Troy was finally burned to the ground, and the Greeks took back their queen.

Troy - where's Troy?

FACT: We're pretty sure it's in Turkey. The remains of a city have been discovered that was inhabited for thousands of years. It was destroyed several times, and fits the description of the legendary city.

Maybe bits of this story are true. But we'll probably never know for sure about the details.

Hmmm! So if Mycenae was real and Troy was real - does that mean the whole story's real?

# THE FABULOUS CITY

**W**hat we know about very ancient Greece is as soupy as soupy can be.

But then around 3,000 years ago, the soup began to disappear.

Did a giant drink it? Did the bowl crack, so the soup leaked out on the table?

Don't be stupid! There wasn't really any soup.

It was around this time that the Greeks invented their own alphabet, started trading with lots of faraway countries, made loads of money, created their own heroes and began telling long adventure stories about them.

Families grew bigger, more people survived into old age, and soon there wasn't enough room for everyone. So Greek adventurers began doing the same thing as their heroes – sailing to foreign lands and setting up cities there.

It's just a way of saying that about 750 BC we start being able to understand what was happening in Greece more clearly.

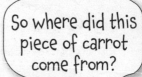

So where did this piece of carrot come from?

But however far away from Greece they lived, there was one city back home they always remembered. It was a city so famous and so beautiful it made people proud to be Greek. And it was called ... **Athens!**

## Once upon a time . . .

. . . in the long-ago days of myth and legend, the goddess Athena looked down from her home, Mount Olympus, on to the land below. Greece was a hot and rocky place. Its islands were bleached and barren, its mountains were high and it was starved of fresh water. All of it, that is, except for one small but beautiful triangle of green rolling hills surrounded by a dazzling blue sea – the land of Attica.

'This will be my land, and I will protect its people,' thought Athena, and floated down to Attica to tell everyone her plan.

But the gods of Greece were an argumentative bunch, and no sooner had she drawn breath than a vast waterspout rocketed out of the sea, and on its crest, riding a giant tuna fish, appeared her Uncle Poseidon, god of the oceans.

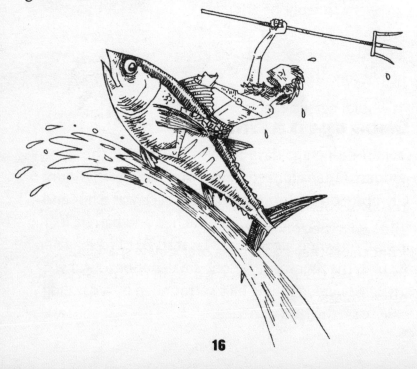

'Leave these people be!' he roared, 'for I will be their protector.'

But Athena wasn't having any of that. She stamped her foot, and an earthquake shook the land.

Poseidon seized the enormous waterspout in his mighty hands, bundled it into the shape of a storm cloud, hurled it into the air and drenched the Atticans in torrents of rain.

'Excuse me!' shouted a particularly brave young Attican (and he had to shout very loud so he could to be heard over the thunderous storm). 'Shouldn't we be allowed to choose who our protector will be?'

And as both gods seemed too surprised to reply, he added, 'Maybe if each of you gave us a really good present, it would help us decide.'

Excuse me!

'It would,' agreed the other Atticans furiously nodding their heads. 'It definitely would.'

Next morning they awoke to the sound of bubbling water, and when they opened their front doors they could see a brand-new sparkling fountain in the shape of a big tuna in the middle of the town square.

'This must be Poseidon's gift,' they said. 'How handy! Fresh water whenever we need it!' and they raced to the fountain with their cups and mugs and saucepans, and started to drink.

'Bleughhh!' they went. 'It's salt water! That's disgusting!'

'I'm going to be sick behind this little tree,' said the brave young Attican.

'What little tree?' demanded his sister. 'There's no tree here.'

But she was wrong. There was now. It was Athena's present. It had olive-coloured leaves and olive-coloured berries, and was in fact an olive tree.

'Olive oil!' exclaimed the brave Attican, quite forgetting how sick he'd been feeling. 'That's what we'll make from now on. We'll rub it on our bodies to keep our skin smooth, we'll cook with it to stop our onions from burning, we'll make perfume with it so our armpits don't smell, and we'll burn it in our lamps so we can see at night. What an amazing present!'

'Thank you, Athena!' shouted the Atticans. 'In return we'll call our town Athens, and we shall be known as the Athenians.'

Up on Mount Olympus Athena smiled. From now on she'd make sure Athens was the most powerful, happening city the Greeks had ever seen.

## LOVELY OLIVE OIL

The Athenians loved olive oil. They even gave it as prizes in their athletic games. Winners of chariot races took home 5 tons of olive oil – that's more than ten thousand bottles!

# THE GROWTH OF ATHENS

Athens was built round a steep, rocky outcrop called the Acropolis.

Back in the days when the Greeks first started living in the area, they'd lived next to this big hill, so that if any enemies approached they could escape up to the top of it and throw stones down on them.

Then the early kings of Athens built a palace fortress on the Acropolis, and from it they ruled the rest of Attica.

But by the eighth century BC there was no longer any need for a palace – because Athens no longer had a king . . .

Normally in the Ancient World you were ruled by a king or a queen who made all the decisions and nobody argued with them. If you didn't have a big shiny crown on your head you had to shut up and do what you were told.

But the Athenian noblemen got fed up with having a king telling them what to do all the time, and decided to try something else instead.

First they became an '**aristocracy**'. The richest, poshest people in Athens, the aristocrats, took over running the city.

'Aristocrats' comes from the word 'aristoi' meaning 'best people' – because they thought they were better than everyone else.

But this was only slightly better than having a king – instead of one rich upper-class loudmouth being in charge, now there were several!

Then they tried being a '**tyranny**'. A series of rulers called 'tyrants' came along. They offered to kick out the aristocrats and do lots of nice things for the poor people of Athens if they helped the tyrants to seize power. At first this seemed like a good deal. Unfortunately, not all the tyrants kept their promises. A lot of them were really mean! And once they were in power, it was difficult to get them out!

Tyrant comes from 'tyrannos', meaning an illegal or oppressive ruler – not much fun, then!

Finally a politician called Cleisthenes (pronounced 'Klice-thin-knees') came up with a brilliant idea. He told the Athenian men that if they joined up with him and fought off the latest tyrant, he'd give them a say in how the city was run.

Oi, put some clothes on!

22

23

And sure enough the Athenians won the battle, kicked out the tyrant, and Cleisthenes' new way of running things was put into place. The Greeks had to make up a new word for this new system, and they called it '**democracy**' meaning 'government of the people'.

## STIG'S BRILLIANT GREEKS NO. 2: THE GREEK WHO WAS BRILLIANT AT DIFFICULT SUMS

Pythagoras said there was no such thing as the perfect sausage. He thought every sausage in the world was slightly different, and every one of them was slightly wonky in some way or other. None of them was perfect, and the same was true of every chicken, every cup, every spider and every hat. In fact the only things that were perfect and always stayed the same were numbers. The number 6 for instance was never 5 or 6 ½, it was always plain old 6. He reckoned this made numbers the most important thing in the universe, and were the secret behind everything else. In fact he got so excited about numbers that he invented sums that are still used by scientists today, two and a half thousand years later. His followers thought he was pretty cool; they even set up a secret society to practise what he taught them.

But he also believed that when humans died, they were born again as animals, and once when he heard a dog barking, he thought it was the sound of his dead friend – maybe he needed to get out more!

## WHAT A BIG LADY!

The first temples on the Acropolis were little plain ones, but as Athens grew richer, wealthy people paid for them to be rebuilt bigger and better.

Until in 450 BC, the Athenians dragged more than 20,000 tons of gleaming white marble up to the top of the hill and built their biggest and best temple yet. They called it the 'Parthenon'.

No expense was spared: it would have cost you one silver talent to buy a massive warship – the Parthenon cost 469 talents!

It's still there in Athens, but it's been knocked about a bit.

The roof was held up by 48 giant columns. It was decorated by the best artists in Greece and inside was a 40-foot statue of the goddess Athena . . . Just imagine how freaky it would be to stand in front of a statue the size of a four-storey building!

What's more, the statue was covered in gold – another 44 talents' worth!

The Parthenon is ancient Greece's most famous monument and it's still standing in Athens today – although some bits have gone missing (including all the gold), and the statue isn't there any more . . .

## LOSING YOUR MARBLES

In the 1800s, a British aristocrat called Lord Elgin was in Athens and, being a bit of a fan of ancient Greece, he went to take a look at the Parthenon. He liked it so much that he wanted to take a bit home with him. So he did (back then you didn't argue with a Lord). In fact he took more than a bit – he hired a team of blokes to dismantle massive chunks of the marble temple and ship them back to Britain.

When people suggested that this might be stealing, he said that the Greeks hadn't been looking after it properly and that really he was doing everyone a favour by 'rescuing' some of it . . . so that was all right then.

Elgin sold the bits he'd taken to the British Museum. They're now called the 'Elgin Marbles', and you can go and see them if you're in London. Lots of people are very cross about all this and the Greek government has spent years trying to get them back! In fact they've got a beautiful empty glass room in the New Acropolis Museum of Athens, just waiting for all the bits to be returned.

# PICNICS ON THE PNYX

Not far from the Acropolis was a smaller hill called the Pnyx, and it had a large open-air theatre cut into its top.

The word 'Pnyx' means 'crowded', because every few weeks thousands of Athenians would make their way up the hill at dawn, carrying picnics and comfy cushions. They'd all squeeze through the narrow entrance, past the guards on the gate and into the theatre. When it was full, red security ropes were pulled across the street up to the hill to stop any more people getting through.

Your name's not on the guest list, sorry.

You're not getting in wearing sandals.

## STIG'S BRILLIANT GREEKS NO. 3: THE GREEK WHO WAS BRILLIANT AT MAKING PEOPLE BETTER

The ancient Greeks thought illnesses were a punishment from the gods.

I knew this would happen! It's because I forgot to sacrifice to Poseidon.

Oh no! I must have upset Athena.

Serves me right! It's because I stuck my tongue out at one of the priestesses.

But then Dr Hippocrates came along, and he thought all this stuff about the gods was rubbish.

From now on Greek medicine was all about looking after your patients, being nice to them and making sure their wounds were clean and sterile.

Mind you, not everyone believed Hippocrates was right.

In fact one thing that might put you off Hippocrates is that he thought it was a good idea to eat other people's earwax!

The crowd at the 'Pnyx' didn't turn up to see their favourite band or watch a show. No. They were coming to vote!

The Athenians loved voting; that was the way they decided how their city should be run.

Not everybody could take part – slaves, women, foreigners and children didn't get a vote.

But that still left at least 30,000 people!

Of course not all 30,000 turned up every time there was a vote. Lots of them had work to do, lived too far away or simply couldn't be bothered.

Usually only about six thousand attended . . . but that's still a massive amount of people.

# HOW TO GET RID OF AN ANNOYING PERSON

When anyone became too powerful or irritating, the Athenians had a special system for getting rid of them. They wrote the name of the person on broken pieces of pottery called 'ostraka' (the ancient Greeks used these instead of scraps of paper, because in those days paper was really expensive and came all the way from Egypt), and put them in an urn.

If the annoying person got more than six thousand votes they had to leave the city for ten years. If they came back before their time was up, they were executed.

Is there anyone you'd like to get rid of like that?

## THE DREADFUL IRON COLLAR

If you committed a serious crime in Ancient Athens you went before a jury – just like today except instead of twelve people, Athenian juries had *five hundred* people on them! They'd listen to the speeches made by the defendant and the accuser, then they'd vote by dropping metal discs in one of two jars, depending on whether they thought the person was innocent or guilty.

## WHAT TIME IS IT?

Speeches were often timed to make sure everyone got an equal say. The Greeks did this using clocks made of water! I know water and clocks don't normally go together; if you pour water into a clock, it'll stop!

But the Greeks didn't use the type of clocks we have today. They took a small clay pot and put a little hole in the base. Then they filled it with water. As the water leaked out, the level went down and revealed lines drawn on the inside of the pot, which told you how much time had gone by. Clever, eh?

If you were found guilty you could face exile or death. Exile meant you were banished from the city. The Athenians thought Athens was so great that having to live anywhere else was a truly terrible punishment!

But not as terrible as being forced to drink poison or being fastened to a big board by an iron collar round your neck, and having the collar slowly tightened until you were strangled to death. These were both common forms of execution and compared with them, exile probably didn't seem so bad.

# HOW TO MAKE A NAME FOR YOURSELF

| CRIME | PUNISHMENT |
|---|---|
| Lazing about too much | DEATH! |
| Looking weird | DEATH! |
| Yawning three times | DEATH! |
| Ignoring a cat | DEATH! |
| Murder | DEATH! |
| Stealing a cabbage | DEATH! |
| Stealing a sprout | DEATH! |
| Pretty much anything | DEATH! |

In 621 BC before democracy was invented, a ruler of Athens called Draco had a clever idea. He decided to write down all the laws and put them up where everybody could see them. That way everyone would know what the law was.

Unfortunately, once he'd written them out, people started to wish he hadn't. Draco's laws were really harsh. The punishment for stealing a cabbage was death. The punishment for 'idleness' was death. In fact the punishment for nearly everything was death.

Even today, thousands of years later, really severe laws are still called draconian . . . well that's one way to make yourself famous!

# DIFFERENT PLANETS

**B**oys and girls in ancient Greece might as well have lived on different planets!

Even as babies they were treated differently. Baby boys were treasured possessions, while baby girls were often chucked out on the street at birth.

Oh waah! I'm a girl!

Greek parents had the right to get rid of any kids they didn't want. If a baby was sick or unwanted, it was taken somewhere far away and ditched. Sometimes a nice rich childless couple would come along, find the baby and adopt it . . . but most times they didn't.

Greek parents nearly always wanted a boy – because a boy would probably grow up to be strong and rich and look after his parents when they were old and doddery. Girls, on the other hand, weren't allowed to earn money, and were likely to get married and look after somebody else's doddery parents. So their parents didn't think they'd be much use to them!

Even if your mum and dad chose to keep you and not chuck you out, life didn't get much better for girls . . .

## STUCK AT HOME

Girls in Greece spent most of their life stuck at home. They weren't even allowed to go shopping! Just imagine if you'd been an ancient Greek girl – what would you have done on Saturdays?

So while Greek men spent lots of time outdoors going to work, hanging out with their mates, buying stuff and generally running the place, women did the cooking, cleaning and sewing . . . No wonder Pandora opened the box. At least it was something exciting to do!

## OPEN THE BOX!

Ancient Greek men believed women were trouble with a capital 'T'! And they thought it had all started with the very first woman in the world – Pandora.

They said that Zeus – the king of the gods – gave Pandora a box and told her not to open it under any circumstances.

(Which if you ask me was a daft thing to do – everyone knows that when you give somebody a box and tell them not to open it, the first thing they do is try and open it . . .)

So Pandora tiptoed over to the box, looked around to make sure no one was watching her, then very, very carefully opened the box just a tiny bit, and . . .

# BOOOM!!

Every single evil thing – Disease, Crime, Hatred, Envy and all the rest – escaped from it into the world. Terrified, Pandora slammed down the lid, but it was too late – all the evils had been released. The only thing left in the bottom of the box was Hope.

After that, the men decided it would be safer to keep women at home under lock and key, where they couldn't cause any trouble. Although personally I think it was just an excuse so they could go down the pub with their mates. I mean, think about it! Who was the troublesome person in the story – Pandora who opened the box, or Zeus who put all the evils of the world in a box but didn't lock it?

# BURGLARY MADE EASY

The ancient Greeks built their houses out of mud bricks. Mud houses are good because they're cheap to make, but they're bad because their walls are so weak. In fact Greek burglars were called 'wall diggers' because they used to dig through the walls of houses to get inside and nick all the stuff!

But if you managed to keep the burglars away, you could live a very nice life in an ancient brick house. The rooms weren't built on top of one another . They were set out around a central courtyard. Greece was a hot

country even back then, so most families preferred to chill out in the courtyard rather than inside – a bit like having an outdoor living room.

Around the courtyard were lots of different sorts of rooms – kitchens, storerooms and bedrooms. At the front of the house was a dining room, where the head of the family (a man) asked his mates (other men) round for dinner parties. They'd all lie on couches, munch food, talk politics, read poetry, listen to music and get drunk.

Hmm, that looks a bit fishy to me!

### TAKE ONE SQUID

The Greeks had their own celebrity chefs – one called Archestratus (pronounced 'Ark-est-rah-tus') – wrote the first ever cookery book!

Most of this book was about fish. The ancient Greeks did eat bread, beans, fruit and olives, plus the odd kebab or a bit of sausage. But, because so many of them lived by the sea, what they liked eating most of all was fish – and not just fish with fins and tails and little faces, but all types of weird seafood.

In fact they liked fish so much they gave it as presents – the picture on one ancient vase shows a boy bringing his girlfriend an octopus! (Maybe she'd have preferred a bunch of roses or a big box of chocolates . . .)

At Greek dinner parties, men ate with their fingers (knives and forks hadn't been invented yet) and played drinking games like 'kottabos', which involved the diners flicking wine from their glasses and trying to hit a target.

If your mum's Greek and you try this at home and get a bullseye, she'll probably pat you on the head and tell you what a clever darling you are.

If your mum isn't Greek and you try it, she'll probably stop your pocket money for a week and send you to bed without any tea.

Oi! Pack it in!

That's a Greek urn.

## TOTALLY POTTY

With so much food, wine and olive oil around, the ancient Greeks had to find something to put it all in. Clay pots, jugs, cups and vases were the ancient Greek version of our plastic packaging.

Thousands of pieces of Greek pottery survive. The Greeks liked painting pretty pictures on their pots – stories of gods and monsters or scenes of daily life – so they can tell us a lot about ancient Greece.

Today some people pay millions of pounds for a Greek vase! Maybe that's what your old lunchbox will be worth in two thousands years' time!

Women weren't invited to these parties – in fact whenever men came round, all the women and girls were sent to a room at the back of the house and were expected to keep themselves busy doing girly things like sewing dresses, brushing each other's hair, and stroking kittens . . . and whatever else it is girls do!

## GREEK FASHIONISTAS

In fact what women spent most of their time doing was making everyone's clothes (there wasn't a Primark in ancient Greece). This wasn't too difficult as both men and women wore simple loose tunics, pinned up and with a belt around the waist.

You could always jazz your outfit up with a bit of jewellery – women had their ears pierced and wore earrings as well as bracelets, necklaces and anklets.

Greek men often wore a ring with a design on it that could be stamped into clay or wax to seal documents.

**TWO-IN-ONE MANLY RING, CONVENIENT STAMP!**

*Because... ladies love lead*

LEAD

Having a golden tan was really fashionable if you were a man, but women tried to look as pasty as possible and painted their faces with chalk or white lead to lighten their skin.

# HOW TO BE A GOOD BOY . . . IN THE NUDE

Probably the only good thing about being a girl in ancient Greece was that you didn't have to go to school. From the age of six, most boys were sent there to be taught important skills.

## Peewee's List of . . . THINGS GREEK BOYS WERE TAUGHT IN SCHOOL

**1 Really really *really* long poems** – All Greek boys were expected to know the works of Homer (no, not Simpson – the original Homer we told you about on page 5). His most popular poem was about the war between the Greeks and the Trojans. It's over 15,000 lines long and would have taken about 24 hours to recite from start to finish (without a loo break) . . . Now that's what I call a long poem. That might seem impossible to learn, but it's full of people being killed in battles – and there's nothing like blood-spurting, spine-ripping, eye-popping violence to get boys learning poetry.

**2** **Naked PE** – Greek boys had to be strong and athletic, because they'd probably become soldiers when they were older. They went to gyms, where they were taught wrestling, running, jumping, discus and javelin throwing. But they couldn't get out of it by saying they'd forgotten their gym kit, because they had to do their exercises naked! Imagine having to strip off every time you did PE!

Erm . . . let's see what's happening over here . . .

What? I'm not bothered.

**3** **How to play a lyre** – The Greeks loved music, and most boys were expected to be able to bash out a tune on a lyre – an instrument that was a bit like a little guitar made of a tortoise shell with strings of twisted sheep gut. If you could sing a bit too, that was even better. We don't know what Greek music sounded like, but a bunch of school boys twanging animal guts doesn't sound great to me.

If running around naked, reading poetry and playing instruments didn't appeal to you – well, tough. Greek parents employed a slave called a 'paidagogos' (which means 'child leader' in Greek) who took you to school and made sure you paid attention!

## SLAVING AWAY

How many times have you wished you had a slave to do everything for you? . . . Well, you'd have loved living in ancient Greece.

Most families had one or two slaves to help around the house. Today we've got machines to help us, back then they had slave-operated devices . . . Instead of a vacuum cleaner you had a slave with a broom, instead of a dishwasher you had a slave with a sponge, instead of a microwave you had a slave with a cooking pot, and instead of a TV you had a slave in a box in the corner of the sitting room pulling funny faces . . . (OK, I made that last one up.)

Some Greeks sold their children into slavery for money (guess which children they were more likely to sell? Correct . . . The girls). But often slaves came from outside Greece – the Greeks would win a war and capture the defeated enemy along with their wives and children.

Sometimes slaves were treated quite well – they'd get decent food, a bed and took part in family occasions. But don't be fooled; it wasn't a total jolly. They couldn't go out, get married or have children without their master's permission and they were whacked if they misbehaved.

Slaves also did other jobs; some were teachers and shopkeepers, others worked in factories, farms, and on board ships.

Most slaves had to work unbelievably hard, all day and into the night, seven days a week. But the ones who got the very worst deal were those who worked in Athens's silver mines. 30,000 of them slaved away underground getting silver out of the rock, dragging it up to the surface and washing it. Not only was it back-breaking work but the silver was mixed with lead – which is toxic – so any slave who worked there long enough died of lead-poisoning. Which really sucked.

While their brothers went to school, girls were taught how to cook and clean. Parents were so keen to get their daughters off their hands that they'd often picked out a future husband for them by the time they were six years old.

At fourteen, girls got married and went to live with their husband's family! Still at least it was a chance to leave the house . . .

Except once she was married, the only job a Greek girl had was to start popping out (boy) babies as soon as possible.

## STIG'S BRILLIANT GREEKS NO. 4: THE GREEK WHO WAS BRILLIANT AT THINKING

Thinking's easy, isn't it? We all do it – even really stupid people. But how do you actually think? How do all those thoughts come into your head? How do you know everything isn't a dream? What does 'happy' mean?

Most people hadn't given this sort of thing a moment's thought until Socrates (pronounced 'Sock-rat-ees') and his mates came along. He was a short ugly-looking man who was always criticizing the rich nobles, but the rest of the Athenians liked him and made him a judge. Eventually though, in order to shut him up, he was put in prison and found guilty of messing with the minds of the young people of Athens. He was sentenced to death, given a cup of deadly poison, drank it and died.

*Thinking, thinking, thinking...*

*Hmmm...*

No one remembers the Athenian nobles any more, but the thoughts of Socrates are still with us today.

## THAT'LL BE TWO AND A HALF GOATS PLEASE . . .

The silver mined by slaves was used to make coins. In fact the Greeks were among the very first people ever to have money.

And if you're thinking 'So what?' then you've never thought about how useful money is . . . and not just for buying chips on the way home.

Ever wondered what people did before they had coins?

**Answer:** They used goats. Well, not just goats . . . they used all sorts of things – they traded animals or crops for other things they needed (like metal tools or a nice kebab). But let's use goats as an example.

There were lots of advantages to using coins rather than goats:

- Goats are difficult to carry around in your pocket.

- Not everyone wants a goat.

- Goats don't have their value written on them – so it's difficult to agree what one goat is worth.

- The average lifespan of a goat's 15 years. After that you need a new goat.

So coins were invented instead. And pretty soon the Greeks realized that they were useful for another reason as well. They already stamped a picture on their coins to show where

they were made, so why not send a message at the same time?

For example the Athenians started stamping pictures of an owl (the symbol of Athena) with wings outstretched holding some olive leaves on their coins. This was a way of telling everyone that Athens was powerful, victorious in battle and peace-making. In other words . . . we're nice guys but don't mess with us.

# Jojo's List of . . .
# FIVE GREAT
# GREEK INVENTIONS

The Greeks weren't just great at making up stories, and having brilliant thoughts. They were also seriously good inventors.

Next time somebody asks you what's so great about the Greeks you can wow them with this top five list of amazing things the geeky Greeks invented . . .

**The First Computer** – In 1900, divers found a strange object in an ancient shipwreck under water off the Greek island of Antikythera (pronounced 'Ant-i-kith-ear-a'). It was a machine about the size of a shoebox made of lots of little rusty metal cogs and gears.

Experts think it was made by the Greeks to calculate the movement of the planets. Which technically makes it the first computer ever invented!

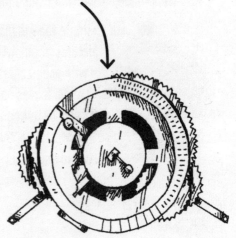

**Catapults** – Catapults are weapons that fire missiles (arrows, stones or even sometimes cows) at an enemy a long way away. The word comes from the Greek meaning 'shield piercer'. The Greeks designed massive powerful catapults – some of which were wound up and then released two missiles at once!

**The Alarm Clock** – Around 250 BC, the teacher Plato designed a water-clock with an alarm to help his students arrive on time to his lectures! It was made of a pot, which slowly filled up with water. When the level of water reached the top, it tipped a bowl of lead balls on to a copper plate and made a ringing sound!

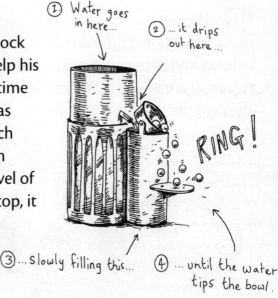

① Water goes in here...

② ...it drips out here...

RING!

③ ...slowly filling this...

④ ...until the water tips the bowl.

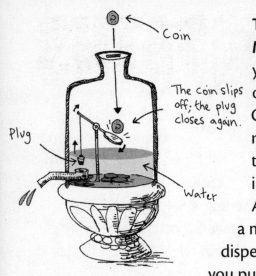

Coin

The coin slips off; the plug closes again.

Plug

Water

**The Vending Machine** – Next time you're getting a packet of crisps or a can of Coke out of a vending machine, just thank the Greeks! The Greek inventor Heron of Alexandria designed a machine that would dispense holy water when you put a coin in a slot. But it wasn't for drinking, it was for washing your hands before you went to worship at the temple!

**Flamethrower** – This was a hollowed-out log, with a metal pipe running through it. At one end was some bellows and at the other was a cauldron full of flaming material. When you pumped the bellows, the air shot through the tube and blew fire at your enemy!

# PSYCHOPATHS

Stand by to meet the craziest bunch of psychopaths ever to call themselves Greek.

Basically take everything you've read about Athens and forget it. Unlike Athens, there was another city that didn't produce great thinkers, politicians and artists. The people of this city thought that swanky buildings like the Parthenon were a big fat waste of money and that thinking great thoughts was for losers.

Grrrrrr!

Their city was called Sparta, they were the Spartans and what they believed in was WAR and BATTLES and BLOOD.

# THE SIEGE OF TROY

One thing the Spartans did share with the Athenians and the other Greeks was their love of the story of the Trojan War – because (a) it was a story about a war and the Spartans loved war, and (b) it was a story that featured . . . da da dahhh . . . yes, the Spartans. The whole Trojan War had supposedly kicked off because Helen, the beautiful wife of the King of Sparta, ran off with the son of the King of Troy.

The King of Sparta, Menelaus (pronounced 'Men-eh-lay-us') joined up with all the other kings of Greece and launched an attack on the city of Troy. The siege of Troy went on for ten long years until the Greeks came up with a clever plan.

They pretended to sail away, leaving a giant wooden horse on wheels as a gift for the Trojans (don't ask me why a big wooden horse is a suitable gift . . . nobody ever explains things like that in stories). But hiding inside the horse were thirty Greek soldiers.

The plan went perfectly – the Greeks pretended to leave and the Trojans opened the gates, saw the horse, thought it was the most terrific present they'd ever seen and pulled it inside the city. Then in the middle of the night, the soldiers crept out of the horse and opened the gate to the Greek army, who burned Troy to the ground, killed lots of Trojans and took the rest away as slaves.

Lessons from the story of Troy:

**Don't mess with the Greeks.**

**Laying siege to a city takes a *long* time.**

**If someone ever leaves a giant wooden horse on your doorstep, call the police.**

The Spartans were so proud of their role in the Trojan War (and the fact their king started it) that in 500 BC they built a shrine to King Menelaus and his wife Helen.

Spartan women visited the shrine to pray they'd be as beautiful as Helen. Spartan men went to pray that they'd be brave and mighty warriors like Menelaus.

Right, got me hat . . . Don't think I need anything else . . .

All Spartan men wanted to be brave – that's what being a Spartan was all about. They trained themselves up to be the most disciplined, awe-inspiring, unbeatable, make-your-enemy-wet themselves-and-run-away soldiers the world had ever seen.

And that meant that the whole of Sparta became one big military training camp . . .

Anything that got in the way of your training was banned – Spartan men didn't farm or fish, they didn't make things or trade with foreigners.

There was a small snag to this plan . . . it meant they didn't have any food. Hmmmm . . .

Well, luckily the Spartans had thought of this. They had people to do all the farming and fishing and making things for them! Slaves . . . lots and lots of slaves.

This wasn't the cushy type of slavery you got in Athens. This was proper slavery. Most people would rather have eaten a barrel of wasps than have been a slave in Ancient Sparta.

## A HELL OF A LOT OF HELOTS

Where did they get all their slaves from?

Well, as the Spartans were pretty good at fighting (being as I think I mentioned the most disciplined, awe-inspiring, unbeatable, etc., etc., soldiers the world had ever seen), they went off and conquered a whole population of people living nearby and enslaved them.

These people were called the 'helots' (which meant 'captives') and they had to farm the land and do all the everyday jobs, so that Spartan citizens could carry on with their military training.

There were hundreds of thousands of helots in Ancient Sparta. In fact there were so many that they outnumbered Spartans by 10 to 1. This made the Spartans nervous – they were always worried about what would happen if the helots all got together and decided to revolt.

So helots were kept firmly under the thumb. In Ancient Sparta it was recommended that you beat your helots soundly at least once a year – even if they'd done nothing wrong – just so they knew who was boss!

There was even a special event each autumn when young Spartans were encouraged to go out at night and murder every helot they came across – which helped young Spartans get better at killing and kept helot numbers down at the same time!

## WE'RE COMPLETELY SECRET

Maybe the Spartans weren't quite as weird and psychopathic as we believe. The trouble is they were really secretive, and hardly wrote anything down about themselves. So every story we know about them comes from people who didn't live in Sparta, or were the Spartans' bitter enemies . . . but I still wouldn't want to bump into one on a dark night!

# SPARTAN LESSON 1: HOW TO KILL

As you've probably gathered by now, the Spartans had some odd ideas about the key skills a young boy needed . . . like the ability to sneak around at night and murder innocent people.

You might think you've got it tough – but that's only because you don't know what boys in Ancient Sparta had to go through.

First off, just as in Athens, any unwanted Spartan children were abandoned. Except that in Athens you might be left in a place where some kindly person could find you and adopt you . . . but in Sparta you were thrown over a cliff.

Dad's says he's taking me for a picnic . . . I've got a bad feeling about this . . .

There was a ravine a few miles outside Sparta called the 'place of rejection', and it wasn't a picnic spot! Babies who the Spartans thought were too sick or weak to be any use were taken there and chucked down it.

PLACE OF
REJECTION
No Picnics

## STIG'S BRILLIANT GREEKS NO. 5: THE GREEK WHO WAS A BRILLIANT GENERAL

A few nights before Pericles (pronounced 'Perry-cleese') was born his mum dreamed she was about to give birth to a lion. Later his fans said this was a prophecy which foretold what a terrific fighter he'd become. But his enemies reckoned it just meant he was going to be a big-head!

Pericles became Sparta's greatest enemy, but his most famous victory wasn't really a victory at all. The mighty kingdom of Sparta decided to attack Athens. A lot of Athenians wanted to fight back, but not Pericles; he knew no one could beat the Spartan army. So he built enormous walls round Athens and told all the people of Attica to pack up their things and hide behind them.

Don't be frightened, I'm 'armless!

When the Spartans arrived they destroyed every little Attican town and village, but they couldn't get inside the big city. It was a terrible time for Athens, but Pericles was a brilliant talker as well as a brilliant fighter. He persuaded the Atticans not to surrender, and when the Spartan army finally gave up and went home, Pericles sent the Athenian navy out to smash the towns which had supported Sparta.

Exactly the same thing happened the following year, but this time it was even worse because a dreadful disease broke out in Athens and a lot of people died, including Pericles' two sons. But once again the Spartans left Athens without having conquered it, and Pericles' navy annihilated the Spartan allies.

Pericles was incredibly popular. He looked after the poorest Athenians; he even gave them free tickets to the shows in Athens's big theatre. He filled the city with magnificent buildings, some of which are still standing today over two thousand years later.

His enemies said he was arrogant, a swindler and not nearly as great as everyone else thought he was. But he won nine trophies for his skills as a general, and showed the whole world that, though Sparta might have had a superb army, the Athenians were smarter, and were determined not to be defeated by their arch-rival.

At seven years old, all Spartan boys were sent away from home to be turned into soldiers.

Most of their time was spent learning how to kill – but you'd also be taught a bit of reading (so you could read books about killing), maths (so you could count the numbers of people you'd killed) and music (to kill to).

To toughen them up, each boy was given only one piece of clothing to wear (a simple cloak . . . dyed red to hide the spatters of blood you were bound to get all over it), and made to sleep rough outside even in winter.

Food was rationed, and boys were expected to steal to get extra food. But if you were caught you were severely beaten – although this wasn't to stop you stealing, it was to teach you to be a better thief!

## A LITTLE NUTTER

One Spartan boy was so hungry he stole a fox and hid it under his shirt. Before he could kill it and eat it, he was made to stand in line for an inspection. Rather than get caught stealing, he stood there quietly while the fox clawed and chewed its way into his stomach, until he died. That was the Spartan way.

See, I told you the Spartans were nutters.

# PIG'S BLOOD AND VINEGAR

To celebrate getting to the age of twelve without starving to death, freezing to death or having your insides eaten by a fox, Spartan boys got to take part in a special challenge.

Lots of delicious cheese was laid out on a table, but to reach the table you had to run past a lot of men attacking you with whips . . . I think I'd rather have had a nice party and some cake, wouldn't you?

But you didn't get cake in Sparta. Cake wasn't allowed. Cake was 'fun'.

The food in Sparta was notorious – the most common dish was called 'Black Broth', and it was made of pig's blood and vinegar. One visitor to Sparta joked that having tasted Spartan food, he could understand why they were all so willing to die!

Things weren't that much better when you became an adult. You weren't allowed to get married until you were thirty and you couldn't leave the army until you got to sixty!

## DOUBLE TROUBLE

While other Greek cities got rid of their kings, the Spartans kept hold of theirs. In fact they didn't have just one king . . . they had two! One to lead the Spartan army into battle, and the other to stay at home and look after Sparta.

Two kings meant two palaces, two royal families and twice as many arguments.

Back off!

No, YOU back off!

# HERACLES

The Spartans believed they were descended from the Greek hero Heracles (or Hercules as some people call him). Heracles was the Superman of the Ancient World – half-human and half-god.

People said he was so strong that even as a baby he'd been able to take care of himself. Once, the goddess Hera (Athena's auntie) sent two snakes to kill him in his cot, but little Heracles just grabbed hold of them as if they were toys and strangled them with his baby fists!

When he grew up, Hera picked on him again – she drove him mad and he killed his own children in a frenzy. To earn forgiveness for this terrible crime he was made to carry out twelve really difficult jobs – these are called the 'Labours of Heracles'.

Among them he had to kill a whole bunch of monsters, including a big lion with arrow-proof fur (the 'Nemean Lion'), a nine-headed dragon called the Hydra, and a load of bizarre man-eating birds with metal feathers! He also had to steal loads of stuff – including a belt from the Queen of the Amazons and some golden apples from Zeus himself.

I love going clubbing!

With all that killing and stealing I'm not sure Heracles would make such a great role-model these days, but no wonder the nutty Spartans loved him!

# SPARTAN GIRLS RULE

Being a girl in ancient Sparta was a world apart from a girl's life in other Greek cities. You got to leave the house for a start.

But more than that – just like boys – Spartan girls were taught to be strong and tough, and how to wrestle and throw javelins. They were also fed the same disgusting food and allowed to drink wine just like the boys.

*Young Spartans* by Edgar Degas.

Spartan women could choose who they married – what's more, they didn't usually get hitched until they were eighteen (which was pretty old for girls in ancient Greece). But as wives and mothers it was their duty to make sure their men didn't back away from a fight.

One Spartan wife said to her husband who was going off to war, 'Return carrying your shield or lying on it' – meaning either come back victorious or dead!

[sniff]
Why?

Spartan women were allowed to own their own property and were expected to be able to guard their homes against invaders while their husbands were away.

Yes, Spartan girls were really tough!

Greek men from other cities thought it was dreadful that Spartan women had so much freedom. But they probably didn't say so out loud when they were visiting Sparta – in case any Spartan women overheard them and punched them!

# THE OLYMPIC GAMES

**A**thens, Sparta and the other Greek city-states never stopped fighting and squabbling. A bit like children, they argued about who was best and which city the gods loved most.

To find out, they held games.

I don't mean they spent wet weekends playing Scrabble.

I'm talking about big fancy competitions – music competitions, poetry competitions and athletics competitions . . . basically any opportunity to show off and get a prize at the end.

If you won you could say it was because the gods loved your city best, and all the losers in the neighbouring cities could go kiss your big hairy butt!

The most famous of all these games were the Olympic Games – maybe you might just have heard of them!

Today the Olympic Games are an international event involving athletes from all over the world – but back in ancient times, only Greeks took part. Every four years, the fittest and strongest athletes from all over the country came to compete and win glory for their hometown!

These games were held in honour of Zeus, king of the gods.

Hey, ladies . . . How you doing?

## ZEUS

The Greeks had lots of gods, like Athena, Poseidon and Hera, but the mighty Zeus (pronounced 'Zoose') was ruler of them all.

His father Cronus had been told that eventually one of his children would overthrow him, and so to stop this happening, each time he and his wife had a baby, Cronus ate it up. Finally when his sixth child, Zeus, was born, his wife (who was fed up with all her children being gobbled up) wrapped a stone in a blanket and gave it to Cronus to swallow instead.

Zeus grew up, became king of the gods and rescued his brothers and sisters by forcing his dad to vomit them all up again!

Zeus had lots of wives and girlfriends. He would disguise himself as things like swans, white bulls, eagles, showers of gold and flames of fire in order to romance unsuspecting women!

The result of this was that he ended up as father to a whole host of kids including **Athena**, **Ares** the god of war, and **Aphrodite**, goddess of love.

Dad, stop chatting up women!

# A WONDER-FUL STATUE...

The Olympic games were held at Olympia – a sacred place with a grand temple dedicated to the mighty Zeus.

Inside it was an enormous gold and ivory statue of Zeus sitting on a giant throne. As one visitor said, it looked as though if Zeus had stood up he'd have taken the roof off the temple!

This statue was so impressive it was known as one of the 'Seven Wonders of the World' (a list of the top seven sights all travellers should go and see).

Before the games started, the athletes would pray to Zeus that they would win their competition, and during the games 100 oxen were sacrificed as a way of thanking him for being such a marvellous god!

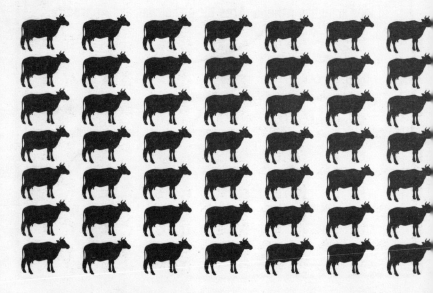

# ON YOUR MARKS . . .

When the Olympics had first started there'd only been one event: a running race which was called the 'stadion' because the athletes had to run a single length of the stadium. Then more events were added because it hadn't been much fun for the spectators to travel for days to get to the games and then only see one short race.

So a there-and-back race was introduced and then a long-distance race. Over time more events were included like wrestling, boxing, long jump, relay races, chariot races, javelin and discus throwing.

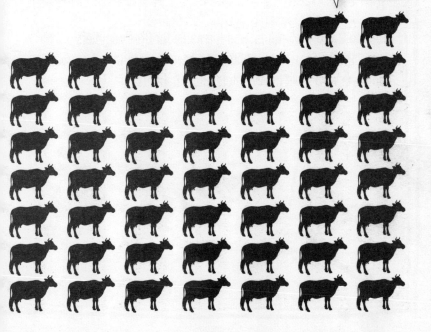

Apparently we're all appearing in the opening ceremony.

**Jojos Guide to ...**
# THREE OF THE MOST DANGEROUS (AND EXHAUSTING) SPORTS IN THE ANCIENT OLYMPICS

**Chariot Racing** – This was the Formula 1 of the Ancient World. Chariots pulled by horses sped up and down a track, careering around a turning post at each end. These posts were known as the 'taraxippus' or 'horse-terror' because it was here that most crashes took place. Accidents were often fatal – the drivers either being crushed by the chariot or trampled by the horses.

**Hoplite Race** – 'Hoplites' was the name for Greek soldiers. Contestants in the Hoplite Race had to run a race in full armour complete with a big heavy shield and a helmet!

**Pankration** – A combination of boxing and wrestling. The word 'Pankration' (pronounced 'Pan-krat-ee-on') meant 'total combat' and there were only two rules – no eye-gouging and no biting. The two competitors kept fighting until one was knocked out, gave up or died!

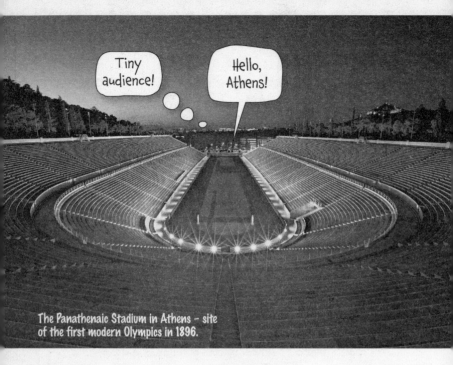

The Panathenaic Stadium in Athens – site of the first modern Olympics in 1896.

The Olympics were a very big deal; over four days the best athletes in Greece came together to take part. This was sometimes tricky because the city-states were often busy fighting one another. So a two-month 'truce' was held while the games were on, allowing people to travel safely to Olympia and back without having to go through a war-zone.

But it wasn't just competitors and spectators who travelled to the games – fast-food sellers, souvenir sellers and gamblers who bet on the races turned up too! In fact it got so crowded that tents were put up for the Olympic village, more tents for the rich spectators and their servants, so the whole place was soon one massive campsite!

Women weren't allowed to take part or watch the events, because all the competitors were stark naked and it was thought that a lot of women gawping at them might put them off.

A mother once tried to get round this rule by turning up disguised as a male trainer. But she got so excited when her son won his race that she revealed her true identity. From then on the trainers had to be naked too – to stop any more women sneaking in!

If I win this, I'll be able to afford some pants!

# SPORTS STARS OF THE ANCIENT WORLD

The athletes who competed in the Olympics were the ancient equivalent of premiership footballers or basketball stars.

They trained hard for years before each event. And, just like sports stars today, they hired personal trainers to help them. Whole books were written with tips on how to train an award-winning athlete, full of the latest workouts and fad diets.

One former champion suggested a diet of nothing but dried figs. I'm not sure about winning races, but if you went on that diet you'd certainly run fast to the toilet!

An ancient Greek gym. Looks a bit draughty.

## BIG MILO

One famous wrestler, Milo of Croton, won SIX Olympic titles! He was supposed to have eaten 20lb of meat, 20lb of bread and drunk 18 pints of wine a day. That's the equivalent of munching your way through 40 massive burgers!

He once trained for the games by lifting a newborn calf and carrying it about on his shoulders every day. As it grew, so did his strength. Eventually it became a full-grown bull, which he continued carrying about until he got fed up with it, then he slaughtered it and roasted and ate it in one sitting!

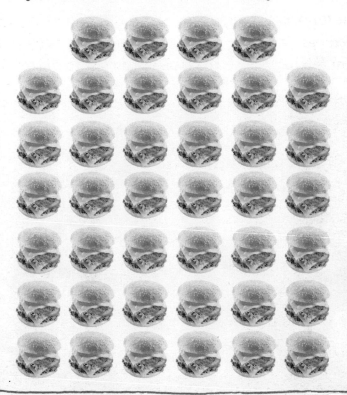

# CHEATERS ALMOST NEVER PROSPER

When all else failed, some athletes resorted to cheating.

The first recorded incident was in 388 BC when a boxer called Eupolus of Thessaly bribed three of his opponents to take a dive, making it look as though he'd knocked them out.

At another games, one runner caught hold of his opponent's hair to slow him down so that he could sprint past him and win!

Cheaty McLoser

Sam Swindle

The officials did their best to put cheaters off – each competition had either a 'whip bearer' or a 'stick bearer' standing by to whack those who broke the rules.

Disgraced cheaters were also forced to pay hefty fines. Each fine paid for another statue of Zeus to be put up near the entrance of the stadium with the cheat's name on it in big letters– so that everybody would know what they'd done. Every athlete had to walk past these statues on their way to the games – how humiliating for the cheater!

I'm not sure they always give their real names . . .

na Sneak

Charlie Cheater

Tricky Ricky

# CHAMPIONES!

If an athlete had trained hard enough (or cheated and managed not to get caught), they might be lucky enough to win. If they were hoping for a big shiny gold cup they'd have been disappointed – all they got was a crown of leaves and a red ribbon. The glory of winning was supposed to be prize enough.

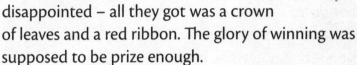

But it was a different story when they got home. They were welcomed back like heroes, given a parade and awarded honours like free meals and a pension for life! Statues of them were put up and poems written about their incredible feats – they became celebrity sportsmen, famous throughout Greece!

## DISCOBOLUS

Greek sculptors loved carving statues of athletes' perfect bodies.

One of the most famous ever made is of an Olympic athlete. We don't know his name – the statue is just called '**discobolus**' which means 'discus thrower' because, er . . . he's throwing a discus.

It's so lifelike that if you stood in front of it you'd be tempted to duck in case the discus took your head off. Which shows how good Greek sculptors were!

# GREECE'S GOT TALENT!

The Greeks didn't just hold competitions to see who was best at running, jumping and throwing things. They also held games that included music, poetry and acting competitions. The most popular of these were the Pythian Games at Delphi, held in honour of the god Apollo.

You're through to the next round!

APOLLON

Just as the Olympic Games began as a single race, the Pythian Games had started off as one singing contest. The competitors had to see who was best at singing a hymn to Apollo, accompanied on a lyre. (See! – all those years at school twanging animal guts eventually paid off!)

Over time other musical and dance contests were included, and eventually acting and poetry reading. You can still see the remains of the huge outdoor theatre built at Delphi in the fourth century BC.

# FART GAGS AND PANTOMIME HORSES

The Greeks invented theatre and everything that went with it – from the props and the scenery to the very first pantomime horse (one picture on a vase shows two men dressed up as a centaur)!

Every town had a theatre and thousands of people would turn up to watch performances. In Athens, even prisoners were sometimes temporarily released so they could go and see a play!

Actors (there were no actresses – this was ancient Greece, remember) wore masks with set expressions to show clearly what their character was thinking (big smiley face = happy; frown = angry, etc., etc.).

As the audience was sometimes a long way away from the stage (as many as 15,000 people turned up to watch some plays), the actors wore big padded costumes and platform shoes to make themselves

visible from a distance. A choir (called a 'chorus') often stood beside the stage to sing about what was happening – so that everyone could follow the story.

There were even special-effects machines. For instance, there was a low platform on wheels which could be pushed around the stage (often to wheel 'dead bodies' on and off stage) and a crane that could make actors fly.

The two main types of Greek play were 'tragedies' and 'comedies'. The tragedies were sad and serious, the comedies involved a lot of stupid fart gags, a lot of making fun of the audience and a lot of filth! I wonder which would be more popular today!

# Jojo's List of . . . FIVE MORE GREAT GREEK INVENTIONS

**The Alphabet** – Did you know that the Greeks came up with lots of the letters we use today? The word 'Alphabet' even comes from the Greek for A and B (Alpha and Beta).

| Αα | Ββ | Χχ | Δδ | Εε |
|----|----|----|----|----|
| Aa | Bb | Cc | Dd | Ee |
| Φφ | Γγ | Ηη | Ιι | Κκ |
| Ff | Gg | Hh | Ii | Kk |
| Λλ | Μμ | Νν | Οο | Ππ |
| Ll | Mm | Nn | Oo | Pp |
| Θθ | Ρρ | Σσ | Ττ | Υυ |
| Qq | Rr | Ss | Tt | Uu |
| Ωω | Ξξ | Ψψ | Ζζ | |
| Ww | Xx | Yy | Zz | |

**Automatic Doors –** Heron of Alexandria designed temple doors which opened automatically. At the same time trumpets started to play, fog was pumped out and statues and metallic birds started

singing . . . which must have completely freaked the worshippers out!!

**Secret Codes –** The Greek historian Polybius came up with a way of sending messages without writing them down. He invented a code which could be sent using fire beacons over long distances – each arrangement of torches signalled a different letter and nobody watching would know what you were saying!

Oi !

What ?

**Death Ray** – The Greek mathematician Archimedes (pronounced 'Arky-mee-dees') was a bit mad. They say he was once sitting in the bath when he had a great idea and was so excited he jumped up and ran through the streets naked, shouting 'Eureka!' ('I've got it!'). One of his most bizarre inventions was the 'death ray' – a series of mirrors which concentrated sunlight on to enemy ships and set them on fire!

**Showers** – And last but not least, the Greeks loved having a good scrub at the public baths and were the first people with showers . . . freezing cold ones!

# SKIRTS VERSUS TROUSERS

In 500 BC everything seemed to be going great for the ancient Greeks.

Their cities were jam-packed with brilliant athletes, world-beating artists and writers, really clever philosophers, genius mathematicians and shrewd politicians.

There was a lot of money to be made, plenty of sun and loads of fish in the sea – Greece was the best place in the world! (OK, so the Spartans were a bit weird but they were good at track events and their army was first-class!)

Hardly anyone realized that a dark cloud was forming on the horizon. A mighty Empire was growing in the East, and it wanted to crush Greece like a bug. This Empire was called . . .

# PERSIA!!

'The Persians' was the ancient name for the people who lived in what is today called Iran in the Middle East. They created one of the largest Empires in history,

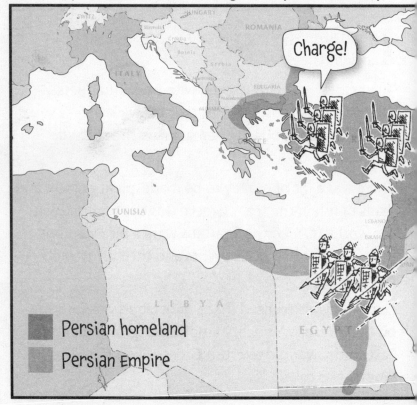

Charge!

Persian homeland
Persian Empire

covering a massive 8 million square miles and three continents! The word 'Persia' actually *means* 'Empire'!

The Emperors of Persia ruled their kingdom with an iron fist – they used a network of roads and thousands of spies to keep an eye on every corner of their Empire. Gold and silver poured in from trade and taxes and was used to build spectacular monuments and an enormous, well-equipped army.

Were they scary?

Yes they were!

## FASHION FORWARD

Did you know? The Persians invented trousers! The Greeks wore a simple tunic, a bit like a T-shirt and skirt sewn together. But the Persian fashion was for baggy trousers tucked into their boots, because it was more comfortable for horse-riding. The Greeks thought they looked ridiculous; as far as they were con

As the Persian Empire expanded westwards, the Greeks started getting a bit nervous.

In 545 BC, the Spartans sent a warning to the Persian Emperor, Cyrus the Great. 'Stay away from Greece,' they said, 'or you'll have the Spartan army to deal with . . .'

When he received this message, Cyrus asked, 'Who are the Spartans?'

He'd never even heard of them!

Somebody kindly explained to him that Sparta was in Greece – a place full of brilliant athletes, world-beating artists and writers, genius mathematicians and so on and so forth . . . at which point, Cyrus immediately added Greece to his list of places to conquer.

Fortunately, Cyrus died before he could pop over there. But in 490 BC his successor, the Emperor Darius, sent an army to invade Attica. The Persian fleet landed a few miles from Athens, near the town of Marathon.

The Athenians had to stop them.

If I wear this dressing gown, no one can laugh at my trousers.

# HOPLITES

Sparta was the only place in Greece with a full-time army, but every city expected its citizens to be able to fight when needed.

You bought your own armour and spear when you left school, and completed your basic training. From then on, whenever your city went into battle it called you up, and you had to get your kit out, dust it off and head out to defend your home city.

Greek soldiers were called 'hoplites', which means 'armoured' – because they were dressed head-to-toe in heavy bronze armour! This included:

**a helmet**

**a breastplate**

**shin-guards**

**a large round shield covered in bronze called a 'hoplon'**

Your shield was the most important bit of your kit. It not only protected you from blows but you could also use it to push forward into the enemy ranks. Hoplites would stand packed close together and overlap their shields forming a shield-wall. Then they'd poke their big spears over the top of their shields into the faces of the enemy.

All this kit was hot and heavy – Greek soldiers couldn't move very fast and they could probably only fight for about 30 minutes before passing out from exhaustion! But it also made them very difficult to kill – swords and arrows barely made a dent in all that armour.

The Persian army outnumbered the Athenians 2 to 1, but the Persians were only lightly armed with bows and arrows and wicker shields. Yes – *wicker* – the stuff people make waste-paper baskets out of . . . I know which side I'd rather have been on!

The two armies met near Marathon and the Athenians were victorious! One writer said that 6,400 Persians died and only 192 Athenians . . . although this could be an exaggeration – the Athenians were so excited at having won, they probably didn't spend a lot of time counting the bodies.

## HOW DOES THE MODERN MARATHON GET ITS NAME?

When the Battle of Marathon had been won, the Athenians sent their fastest runner – a chap called Pheidippides (pronounced 'Fi-dip-e-deez') – to take the news of their victory back to Athens. After legging it 26 miles, the exhausted Pheidippides arrived home, gasped 'We've won' and then dropped down dead . . . Bet he wished the ancient Greeks had invented mobile phones.

Their defeat at Marathon put the Persians off invading Greece . . . but only for a little while.

## THE INVASION OF THE CENTURY

It wasn't long before Darius's son Xerxes ( pronounced 'Zurk-sees') was planning another invasion . . . and this time it was going to be done properly. Xerxes mustered troops from all over the mighty Persian Empire – more than 250,000 soldiers from places as far away as Egypt, India and Africa.

He made sure *nothing* would get in his way – he ordered a bridge to be built over the channel separating Asia and Europe to carry his troops across, and a giant canal was dug to help his fleet of Persian ships reach Greece faster and more easily.

Xerxes was planning the invasion of the century! Everybody was talking about it. Especially the Greeks . . .

Have you heard who's coming?

Those bossy Persians, I know . . .

## 'WATER' LOAD OF RUBBISH

For a long time, people didn't believe that Xerxes really built a giant canal – no sign of it remained and experts didn't think it possible without mechanical diggers.

But using modern technology, scientists recently found evidence of the remains of it buried underground in northern Greece! Over a mile long and wide enough for two ships to pass, the canal must have been dug by hundreds of workers using just shovels and buckets on pulleys.

It allowed the Persian fleet to take a shortcut into the Aegean Sea. But after the invasion it must have silted up and become buried over time.

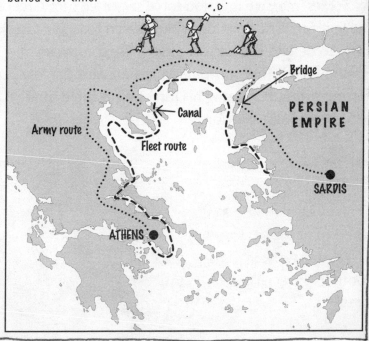

## UNITED WE STAND

The Greek cities held a meeting and decided that the only chance they had of stopping the invasion was to join forces!

Either they stood together or Greece would become a province of the Persian Empire and they'd all have to start speaking Persian and wearing ridiculous trousers.

This time it wouldn't just be Athens doing the fighting: thirty-one Greek cities joined together under the leadership of Sparta.

## THE THREE HUNDRED

As Xerxes' massive invasion force swarmed into Greece, the Spartan King Leonidas volunteered to lead a Greek army to defend the narrow pass of Thermopylae (pronounced 'Ther-mo-pih-lee') to prevent the Persians getting through. Among his forces were three hundred of Sparta's finest warriors.

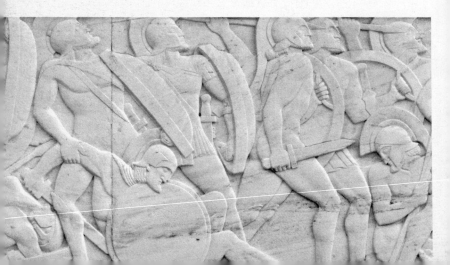

The Persians were about to find out about the Spartans ... the hard way.

Xerxes and his huge army finally arrived at Thermopylae and waited for the little band of Greeks in front of them to retreat ... and they waited ... and waited.

A Persian messenger delivered a warning: 'If you don't go away we will shoot so many arrows at you that it will blot out the sun!'

The Spartan replied: 'So much the better, we'll fight in the shade.'

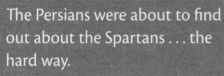

## STIG'S BRILLIANT GREEKS NO. 6: THE GREEK WHO WAS BRILLIANT AT WRITING PLAYS

Once upon a time there weren't such things as plays. There was only a bit of singing and dancing to keep the gods happy. Then people started coming to watch, so little stages were built to make it easier for them to see.

After that poems started being specially written for these little shows, and gradually the whole thing got more and more complicated until . . .

SHOWBIZ WAS BORN!

Ta-daah!

The very first
proper play that
still exists was
written by a playwright called
Aeschylus (pronounced 'Eeska-lus').
Before he became famous he'd been a soldier,
and fought in the Battle of Marathon and the Battle of Salamis.
So not surprisingly some of his plays were about the Persians.

In those days there were competitions all over Greece to find
the most talented performers and writers, and Aeschylus nearly
always won.

He died when he was hit by a tortoise which was dropped by a
flying eagle . . . Honestly! And even though he had been such
a celebrity, his gravestone doesn't mention his success in the
theatre – it just says he fought bravely against the Persians.

Sorry for
dropping in
unannounced,
mate!

The Emperor Xerxes was furious. He ordered his troops to advance and clear the pass – then sat back to watch the action.

What he saw was wave upon wave of Persians crashing against a wall of hoplites. No one had ever seen so many armed men held at bay by such a tiny fighting force. Xerxes threw everything he had against the Greeks but for two days the Persian bodies just kept piling up.

Finally on the third day Xerxes had a lucky break – a Greek traitor came to him and told him about a secret path around the pass.

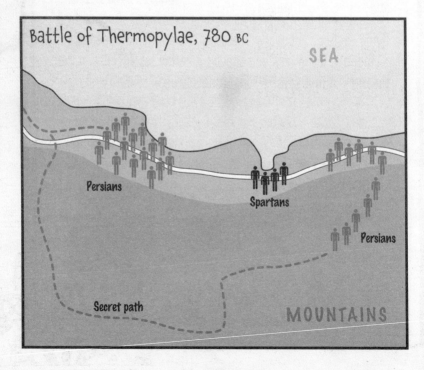

Battle of Thermopylae, 780 BC

SEA

Persians

Spartans

Persians

Secret path

MOUNTAINS

## STIG'S BRILLIANT GREEKS NO. 7: THE GREEK WHO WAS BRILLIANT AT INVENTING HISTORY

The reason that we know so much about what happened in the Persian Wars was that a Greek called Herodotus wrote about it.

He grew up just after these wars had finished – everyone was talking about how surprising it was that Greece had won.

He decided he wanted to write a story about what happened, which in those days meant thinking up a nice long poem full of heroes, heroines, gods and monsters.

But Herodotus didn't want to do that . . . he'd read enough poems at school. No, he wanted to write about what really happened and why. So he travelled the world, talking to lots of people and asking questions like 'Why did the Persians invade Greece?', 'How come they lost?' and 'Why did they wear girly trousers instead of sensible skirts?'

Herodotus was the first 'historian'. After that everyone started asking questions about the past and they haven't stopped since. In fact we've got Herodotus to thank for this very book!

Our hero!

When he heard that they'd been betrayed, King Leonidas ordered most of Greek soldiers to retreat. But to give the others time to get away, he and a small group of Spartans stayed put in order to delay the enemy for as long as possible.

Persian soldiers poured through the little pass and soon the Spartans were surrounded on all sides. They fought to the last. When every spear was broken, they used their swords. When those had shattered, they used their bare hands, until after three days they were all dead.

But it had cost the Persians dearly – they had lost more than 20,000 men!

Now the Persian army swarmed into southern Greece and smashed Attica to bits. Even the mighty city of Athens was ransacked, though its inhabitants had been evacuated to the nearby island of Salamis.

It looked like the Greeks would be completely defeated and they'd have to suffer death and slavery and be forced to wear those daft trousers. But they had one final card to play – the Greek navy was itching for a fight.

And it was in the channel of water off Salamis that the navy made its last stand.

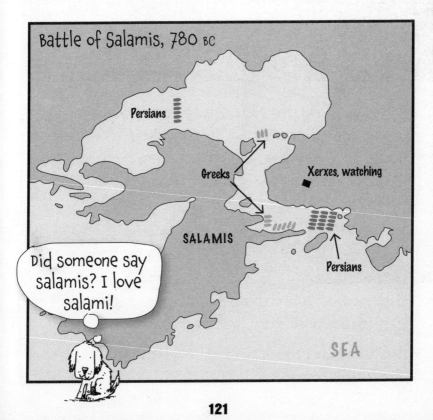

# GREEK SUPER-SHIPS

The Athenians had recently invested in 180 brand-new state-of-the-art battle ships. They were called 'triremes' or 'three-oarers' because there were three rows of oars on each side, powered by 170 oarsmen.

On the front of each ship was a massive wooden battering ram to punch holes in enemy boats, and a pair of big white eyes to make them look extra-scary!

The decks were full of rows of oarsmen; there wasn't any space on board for things like beds or kitchens or loos. So you can imagine the inside of a trireme got pretty disgusting!

Xerxes really wanted to finish the war and get home to Persia. So he sent his fleet of 1,200 Persian ships to wipe those cocky Greeks off the map. Unfortunately for him, there were too many Persian ships for the size of channel – they got all got jammed together!

The Greek triremes picked them off one by one – capturing or sinking over 200!

It was total victory!

Soon the Persians went home and never tried invading Greece again!

So what did the Greeks do next? They went back to fighting each other of course!

# A GREEKISH HERO

**OK** – now we come to Alexander the Great. Alexander lived in the fourth century BC in Macedonia. Macedonia was the kingdom next door to ancient Greece. Now you might be thinking, If Alexander wasn't from Greece then what is he doing in a book about the Greeks . . . ?

If you are thinking that then well done, you're a very intelligent person who will go far and will probably end up being Prime Minister.

The answer is that even though they didn't live in a Greek city-state, the Macedonians still thought of themselves as Greek. They spoke Greek and believed in Greek gods. They even demanded to be allowed to join in the Olympic Games, which was a Greeks-only event. So they may not have been completely Greek, but they were certainly Greek-ish!!

Alexander's dad had been the King of Macedonia. He'd paid for young Alex to have the best Greek teachers who taught him all about Greece.

When Alexander took over from his dad as King, he wanted to carry on spreading 'Greek-ness' around the world. To do this, he started invading other countries and making them part of a single massive Greek-ish Empire.

## THE ONE-EYED KING OF MACEDONIA

Alexander's dad was the famous and fierce King Philip II of Macedonia. He had led the Macedonian army to many victories – he had even lost an eye and had a massive scar across his cheek from being hit in the face with an arrow during a battle!

Philip had turned Macedonia from an insignificant little state on the edge of Greece into a powerful kingdom. The Greeks didn't like Philip much – they thought he was a barbarian in a bearskin who drank too much.

Still, that didn't stop him taking over Greece! One by one he took control of the Greek city-states and made himself 'Commander of the Greeks'.

A small ivory statue
assumed to be Philip II.

## STIG'S BRILLIANT GREEKS NO. 8: THE GREEK WHO WAS BRILLIANT AT BEING ANNOYING

Diogenes was very grumpy. One sunny day Alexander the Great, the most powerful man in the world, came to visit him. The conversation went something like this . . .

I have enormous respect for you, old man. Is there anything I can do for you?

Yes, I can't catch the rays with you standing in front of me. Move out the way!

OK, that was downright rude, but Diogenes' point was that you shouldn't be nice to someone just because they're rich and famous. He thought the worst thing anyone could be was two-faced. He was always shocking people, trying to teach them not to show off. He dressed like a beggar, weed on people he didn't like and even did a poo in the theatre. He was a bit scary and fairly disgusting, but he was very clever and was never frightened of powerful people. A lot of folk learned from him that they didn't need to be in awe of the rich Athenians. But however much he disliked showing off, wasn't he a bit of a show-off himself?

Alexander wasn't called 'Alexander the Great' because he had great hair or was great at doing 1,000-piece jigsaws.

He was called 'Great' because he was good at conquering places . . . in fact he was really, *really* great at it.

Why are there so many images of my lovely hair? Because I'm worth it!

Isn't he gorgeous?

What a hunk!

Huh!

What a show-off!

He made conquering countries look easy: first Persia, then Palestine, Syria, Afghanistan and Egypt were all defeated by Alexander's army. He never lost a single battle! He could conquer places with his eyes shut and one hand tied behind his back.

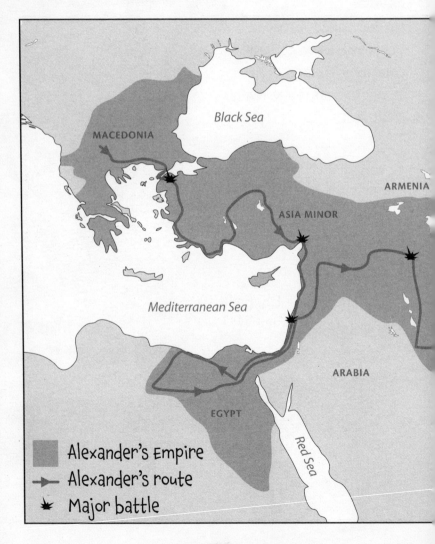

In less than ten years he had conquered most of the Ancient World and created a great big Empire!

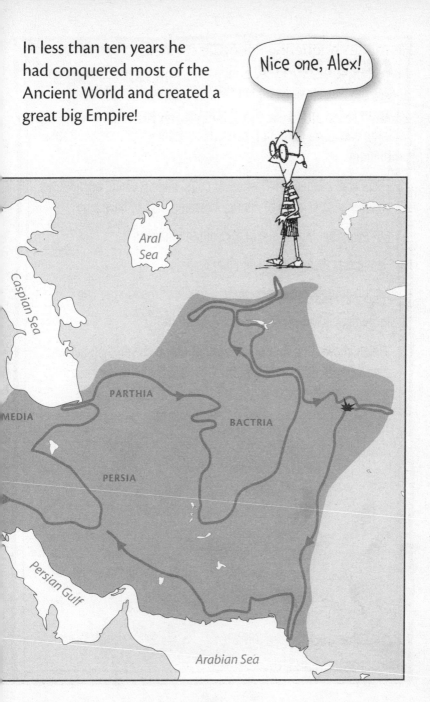

# A KNOTTY PROBLEM

One day Alexander arrived at the ancient city of Gordium in modern-day Turkey. He was shown the famous 'Gordian Knot', a large and ancient knot of rope, which nobody had ever been able to untie.

There was a legend that whoever could undo it would become the conqueror of Asia, so of course Alexander had to have a go.

But even the mighty Alexander couldn't manage it.

So did this mean he'd never conquer Asia?

No, he promptly drew his sword and sliced the knot in two.

Problem solved!

Which shows that Alexander was not only a clever chap but was also a pretty nifty swordsman!

# ARE WE THERE YET?

Alexander's army loved him and would follow him anywhere – even when it meant trudging through a desert wasteland for weeks and weeks, dying of thirst and having to eat your horse.

In 325 BC Alexander began to cross the dreaded Gedrosian Desert. Nobody had ever brought an army through it successfully and he was determined to prove that he could!

To avoid the heat the troops marched at night, but supplies were short and both men and animals started collapsing from thirst and exhaustion. Anybody too sick or tired was left behind – the army had to keep moving to get to the other side of the desert as fast as possible. Some soldiers ended up butchering their own horses and eating them just to stay alive!

Don't even think about it!

Alexander's army finally made it across, but hundreds had died, their bodies left behind to be swallowed up by the desert sands.

## OX-HEAD

Alexander's horse was almost as famous as him.

When Alexander was thirteen, his dad bought a massive black horse with a white star on his forehead. But the horse turned out to be so wild that nobody could ride him. The King told Alexander that if he could tame the horse, he could keep him. To everybody's surprise, Alexander managed it!

But he didn't give his new pet a romantic name like 'Black Beauty' – no, he named him 'Bucephalus' or 'Ox-head' because he had a huge head. He may have been an odd-looking horse, but Alexander loved him very much and rode him everywhere.

Eventually 'Ox-head' was killed in a battle. Alexander was gutted, so he founded a new city on the spot and named it Bucephala. The first (and only) city to be named after a horse!

# THE END OF THE WORLD

Eventually Alexander's army refused to go any further east – they'd reached India and they thought if they went any further they'd fall off the end of the world. (They didn't know there was all of China further east!)

## GOING BANANAS

In India Alexander and his army discovered strange bendy yellow fruit growing on tall trees and they tasted delicious. In fact they were so yummy that the Greeks brought a load of them back home. So it's Alexander the Great that we have to thank for the banana!

Alexander agreed to start heading home.

Unfortunately, he never made it back – he died mysteriously of a fever in 323 BC. We don't really know what killed him – some people say he was poisoned, others think he died of malaria or typhoid fever . . . (or perhaps he just ate a dodgy banana?).

He was only 32 but he had conquered more places than any other person before or since!

In northern India Alexander won a battle against war elephants.
After that his men didn't want to carry on any further.

On his deathbed, his officers came to Alexander and asked him who should take over the Empire he'd created? To which he responded, '*The strongest.*'

So all his generals were left to fight it out among themselves!

In the end they chose to split it up because it was so large – each general took a separate bit of the empire: one took Egypt, one took the lands of East Asia, one took the area of modern Turkey and one took Macedonia. As for the Greek cities – well, most of them went back to fighting among themselves! (What did you expect?)

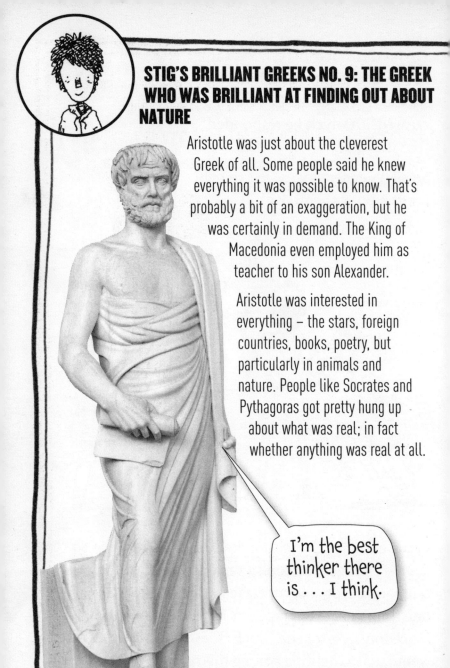

## STIG'S BRILLIANT GREEKS NO. 9: THE GREEK WHO WAS BRILLIANT AT FINDING OUT ABOUT NATURE

Aristotle was just about the cleverest Greek of all. Some people said he knew everything it was possible to know. That's probably a bit of an exaggeration, but he was certainly in demand. The King of Macedonia even employed him as teacher to his son Alexander.

Aristotle was interested in everything – the stars, foreign countries, books, poetry, but particularly in animals and nature. People like Socrates and Pythagoras got pretty hung up about what was real; in fact whether anything was real at all.

I'm the best thinker there is . . . I think.

But Aristotle said he saw real things every day – the rain falling, chickens laying eggs, people sneezing, that kind of thing.

He was good at writing too. People called his words 'a river of gold'.

He wasn't always right. He thought the Earth was the centre of the universe, that heavy objects fall faster than light ones, and that women have more teeth than men.

Blimey!

But he had the courage to tell Alexander the Great that kings and queens were pointless unless they were better behaved than all their subjects put together – and I reckon that makes him not only very smart, but also very brave!

# WE'RE ALL GREEKS NOW

Alexander's massive Empire may not have lasted very long but he brought 'Greek-ness' to the whole world.

During his travels, he had founded more than 70 cities all across his Empire. The generals who took over from him built even more!

Greetings from Egypt

These cities were run by Greeks and had all the things – like gymnasiums, theatres and temples – that Greek cities had.

Pretty soon, lots of Greeks were moving out of Greece and into these new cities – why stick around in boring

Greetings from Sicily

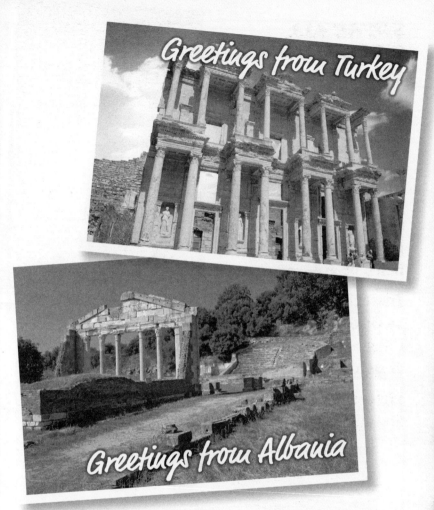

Greetings from Turkey

Greetings from Albania

old Greece when you could live it up in exotic places like . . . Alexandria (named after who? You guessed it) in Egypt?

The Greeks brought with them their language, their fashions, their money and their ideas. Famous scientists, philosophers and artists came from all over the world to study Greek documents in its world-famous library.

## THE LIBRARY OF ALEXANDRIA

In the Ancient World there was no internet, no magazines, no newspapers and no printed books. So if you wanted to find out anything you either had to ask somebody or find a library and look it up in a scroll.

The library at Alexandria was built by one of Alexander's Generals, Ptolemy (pronounced 'Tol-em-ee') in about 300 BC. It was the largest library in the Ancient World. People said it had a copy of every book (or 'scroll') ever written!

The rulers of Alexandria were so proud of their library that they'd do anything to get hold of books for it. Sometimes they stole them off ships visiting the city. Once they asked to 'borrow' a load of rare books from the city of Athens and never returned them!

Great, we've finally got the full set of Tony Robinsons!

142

It would take rather a long time to read every book ever written. Unfortunately, even if you wanted to try it, you couldn't. The library at Alexandria was burned down when the city was attacked and many of its books were lost forever.

It was an accident, I promise!

Which is a real shame – just think of all the stuff that might have been in those books . . . an invention for a time machine perhaps? Or the recipe for the elixir of life? Or maybe just an ancient Greek version of this book?

One of the people blamed for burning down the library was Julius Caesar – the famous Roman general. He attacked Alexandria in 48 BC as part of his campaign to take over Egypt.

## GRACE'S BRILLIANT GREEKS NO. 1: THE GREEK WHO WAS BRILLIANT AT TELLING STORIES

Homer was a blind poet who told really exciting tales . . .

> Hang on! Isn't this the bloke who was *my* Brilliant Greek No. 1?

Well yes, but some people think Homer was a woman. So I'm putting him/her in twice.

> But weren't Greek women supposed to stay at home and not do anything except have babies?

That's certainly what a lot of ancient writers tell us. But it can't have been completely true. There's a woman poet called Sappho whose poems are just as good as any written by the male Greek poets.

There are a lot of smart goddesses in the ancient tales too, like Athena and Artemis, who do all sorts of clever stuff, and you get the feeling their characters were based on the swanky celebs of the time.

We can't prove whether Homer was a Home-him or a Home-her, but there must have been loads of Greek women around who were just as brilliant as the brilliant blokes – we just don't know their names!

Girls are just as clever as boys!

No, you're not. You're as thick as Greek yogurt.

# ROME RULES

The Romans had read about what Alexander the Great had achieved and thought that creating a global Empire sounded like a great idea! So they copied him.

Slowly they started taking over the world – first they conquered Greece and Macedonia, then they moved into Asia and Egypt. All these places became Roman provinces.

Countries that for centuries had been ruled by the Greeks, started to be ruled by the Romans.

But it wasn't the end of Greek-ness . . .

The Romans were big fans of Greek stuff. They took home with them Greek works of art and Greek books; they adopted Greek gods and employed Greek teachers. Some Romans even toured Greece and studied in Athens.

And the Romans passed Greek ideas on to us!

Next time you walk down a street and see a building with lots of fancy columns on the front, next time you go to a **theatre** or **write a story**, next time you use a **calculator**, look at the **stars** or eat a **banana**, next time you **pick up a book** because you're really interested in finding out what's inside it – remember that you're following in the footsteps of the ancient Greeks!

# THE END

So, why were we Ancient Greeks so brilliant? Was it because we had loads of slaves to do all our work, so we could just lie around thinking?

Erm . . .

Was it because we ate lots of fish, and fish is good for the brain?

Erm . . .

Was it because our gods didn't care about us very much, so we had to work things out for ourselves?

Erm . . . Erm . . .
Erm . . . Erm . . .

What was the question again?

# TIMELINE

| | |
|---|---|
| **6500 BC** | The first farmers start to settle down in Greece |
| **3300 BC** | The Sumerians, who lived in modern Iraq, develop writing |
| **3000 BC** | The ancient Egyptian civilization gets going |
| **1500 BC** | A great palace stands at Knossos – could this be the home of King Minos and the Minotaur? |
| **1180 BC** | The Trojan Wars happen (according to some people!) |
| **776 BC** | The Olympic Games begin |
| **740 BC (ish)** | The Greeks develop their own alphabet |
| **700 BC (ish)** | Some Greeks settle in Sicily and southern Italy, while the Etruscans start a little civilization further north in Italy. |
| **621 BC** | Draco the Athenian writes down his very strict laws |
| **610–575 BC** | Sappho knocks out some fantastic poetry, despite being a woman (shock!) |
| **548 BC** | The Temple of Apollo at Delphi is destroyed |
| **534/3 BC** | Thespis becomes the world's first actor, and wins a talent contest in Athens |
| **525 BC** | The Persians take over Egypt |
| **525–500 BC** | Pythagoras gets excited about numbers |
| **520 BC (ish)** | Athenians start making their own coins with owls on |
| **509 BC (ish)** | The Romans kick out the Etruscans and start a new republic |
| **507 BC** | Cleisthenes comes up with a great new idea – democracy! |

| | |
|---|---|
| **490 BC** | The Emperor Darius of Persia sends an army to invade Attica: for 20 years, Darius and his son Xerxes keep trying to bash the Greeks, but eventually have to give up |
| **484 BC (ish)** | Herodotus the historian is born. A few years later, he starts asking some pretty good questions . . . |
| **480 BC** | At the Battle of Thermopylae the Spartans prove how hard they are |
| **460–377 BC** | Dr Hippocrates works on his bedside manner |
| **450 BC** | The Athenians build the Parthenon, a massive marble temple to the gods with a 40-foot-high golden statue of Athena inside |
| **445–429 BC** | Pericles rules Athens, which he turns into a great city (he also sends the Spartans packing, twice) |
| **431 BC** | A major bust-up between Athens and Sparta begins, called the Peloponnesian War |
| **399 BC** | Socrates is ordered to drink poison, and for once he does as he's told |
| **384–322 BC** | Aristotle thinks great thoughts (and also teaches Alexander the Great) |
| **323 BC** | Alexander the Great dies at the age of 32; he's been busy! |
| **300 BC** | Ptolemy builds the Library at Alexandria, which holds over half a million books |
| **200 BC** | By this time, the Romans have conquered the Greeks |
| **1800s** | Lord Elgin swipes some lovely souvenirs from the Parthenon |

# QUIZ

1 Who thought they were the 'best people' in Athens?

2 Where did Elgin put his marbles?

3 What did Hippocrates suggest you do with your earwax?

4 What drew the crowds to the hill called the Pnyx?

5 What clever gadget could the Greeks make with just a pot of water?

6 What did Draco think should happen to lazy people?

7 What was the last thing left in Pandora's box?

8 How do you break into a Greek house?

9 What sort of fishy Valentine might impress an ancient Greek?

10 How did the Athenians kill Socrates?

11 What should you wear for your ancient Greek PE lesson?

12 What did the Athenians put on their coins?

13 What came out of Greek vending machines?

14 What did the Helots do for the Spartans?

15 What colour was a Spartan school uniform?

**16** Which god avoided being eaten by his dad?

**17** What was the Olympic sport of 'total combat' called?

**18** What did the Olympic hero Milo of Croton carry around with him?

**19** What did Archimedes use to make his death ray?

**20** What strange new garment did the trendy Persians wear?

**21** What does the word 'hoplite' mean?

**22** Who was killed by a flying tortoise?

**23** What did Diogenes ask Alexander the Great to do for him?

**ANSWERS** 1) The 'aristoi', or 'aristocrats'. 2) In London. 3) Eat it. 4) Not concerts, not the view – elections! 5) A clock. 6) Death! 7) Hope. 8) Dig through the wall. 9) An octopus. 10) With poison. 11) Nothing at all! 12) An owl with olive leaves. 13) Holy water. 14) Everything – they were their slaves! 15) Red – to hide the bloodstains! 16) Zeus. 17) Pankration. 18) A bull. 19) Mirrors. 20) Trousers. 21) Armoured. 22) Aeschylus the playwright. 23) Move out of the way of the sun.

Tony Robinson's Weird World of Wonders is a multi-platform extravaganza (which doesn't mean it's a circus in a large railway station). You can get my World of Wonders game on line, there's a website, ebook, audio versions, extra stories and bits of weirdly wonderful design, marketing and publicity. In order to get all those things sorted out, I've surrounded myself with a grown-up version of the Curiosity Crew. They are Dan Newman (Design), Amy Lines (Marketing), Sally Oliphant (Publicity), James Luscombe (Digital), Tom Skipp (Ebooks), and Becky Lloyd (Audio). A big thanks to them all; they are committed, funny and extremely cool.

Tony has to say that otherwise they'd stop work and go home!

# Also available in this series

PLAY THE AWESOME WEIRD WORLD OF WONDERS **GAME** NOW AT

WWW.WEIRDWORLDOFWONDERS.COM

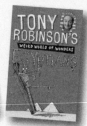

TONY ROBINSON'S WEIRD WORLD OF WONDERS ROMANS

TONY ROBINSON'S WEIRD WORLD OF WONDERS EGYPTIANS

TONY ROBINSON'S WEIRD WORLD OF WONDERS BRITISH